Dedicated To:
My brothers, Ben, Trey & Andrew

Written By: Abigail Gartland

Hello, my name is St. Benedict!

I was born in Italy in the year 480.

I have a twin sister, who is also a saint!

This is St. Scholastica.

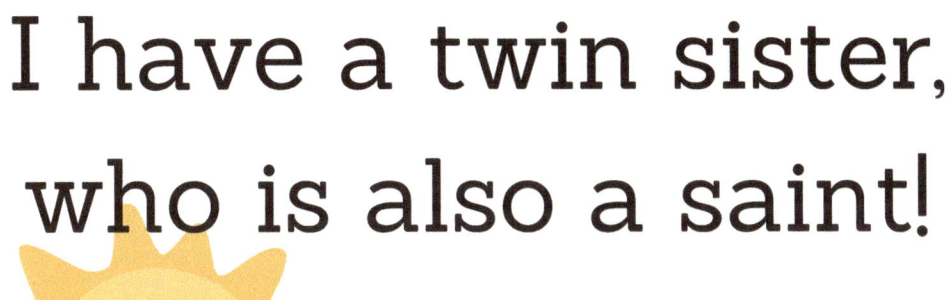

When I grew up, I became a hermit.

I spent all my time alone, and I never saw any people.

After a while, I formed a religious group of men, and we lived in the mountains.

I spent lots of time in quiet prayer.

I wrote my ideas down, and it became a book, *The Rule of St. Benedict.*

This book teaches you how to do many things!

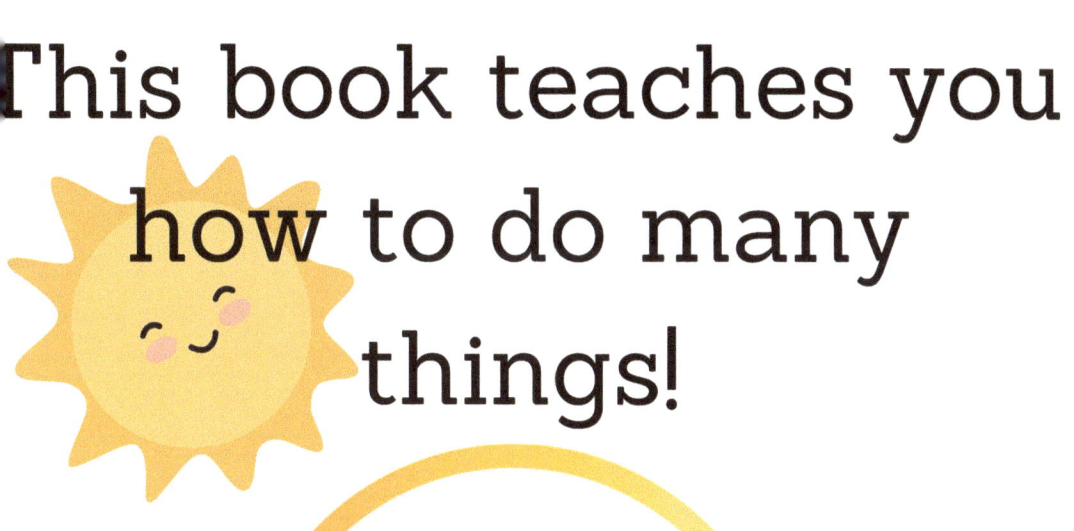

It teaches you how to be kind.

It teaches that everyone deserves to be treated with love.

My book gives good deas for people to live by.

I am the patron saint of students and Europe!

Do you want to be more like me?

You can celebrate my feast day with me on July 11th!

Make sure you are kind and loving to everyone you see.

I pray for you every day of your life.

St. Benedict, Pray for us!

Copyright:

Clipart: © PentoolPixie © LimeandKiwiDesigns
Licensed purchased: 1/10/2024

About the Author
Abigail Gartland

I love the saints and I love my faith. The idea for sharing the stories of the saints with little ones came when my dear friends were expecting their first baby. I wanted to create something as unique and special as our friendship. Each book is dedicated to very special people and groups who have enriched my faith in different ways. I am blessed to write these stories and appreciate the unending support of my family and friends. When I am not writing, I am a middle school teacher. I hope you enjoy these stories. I pray for each and every person who opens one of my books to learn more about the saints.

Abbie

www.ingramcontent.com/pod-product-compliance
Lightning Source LLC
LaVergne TN
LVHW051042070526
838201LV00067B/4896